I AM SUN DRENCHED DREAMS

Mary Chydiriotis

BookLeaf
Publishing
India | USA | UK

Presentation by *BookLeaf* Publishing

Web: www.bookleafpub.com

E-mail: info@bookleafpub.com

ISBN : 9789358361605

First edition 2021

For Marsiale D'Avolio,

My love, my Bouki

'In the presence of kindness, we
flourish. It's that simple, that powerful'

Stephanie Dowrick

ACKNOWLEDGEMENT

I'd like to express my gratitude to everyone at Bookleaf Publishing for creating the #writeyourheartout writing challenge and for publishing my work. Earlier versions of 'Youth ends in time', 'Catch up new normal', 'Lament', 'Sepia stained', and 'Less painful in pieces' were published in The Unprecedented Review, Global Poemic, Garfield Lake Review and Pash Captule.

Photo credit to Brendan Bonsack.

The Melbourne poetry and spoken word scene is thriving due to a dedicated group of individuals who love words and acknowledge their power to move people and create community.

I'd like to acknowledge every poet and performer who courageously steps onto that (Open Mic) stage. Steve Smart for his encouragement and guidance, Annerleigh Pappos for her friendship and generosity, Amanda Anastasi for her advice and wisdom, Alex Jan Margaret Angus, Stuart Barnes, Rob

Black, Amy Bodossian, Brendan Bonsack, Henry Briffa, Eddy Burger, Josh Cake, Edward Caruso, Santo Cazzati, Libby Charlton, Emilie Collier, Angela Costi, Rhonda Crisp, Rochelle D'silva, Cathryn Daley, Koraly Dimitriadis, Jeltje Fanoy, Laura Fisher, Gerard Lewis-Fitzgerald, Ela Fornalska, Misbah, Marty MonStar, Wahibe Moussa, Anthony WP O'Sullivan, Dorothy Poulopoulos, Andrew Raviers, Michael Reynolds, Mary Stone, Kylie Supski, Phu-Linh Tran, Dimitris Troaditis, Carl Walsh and many more for their kindness.

To the incredible Andy Jackson and Alana Kelsall for inspiring me to write poetry.

My poetry, writing and reading groups for providing the nourishment and space to explore language.

My poetry sisters Laura Brinson and Vasilka Pateras for helping sustain me during 2020 and for their collaboration in bringing to life our collection 'Thread'.

I'm blessed to have worked with the best people. Passion aligned with generosity and vision and love. The MRC crew: Stavroula Mavroudis, Franca Pupillo, Cristina Del Frate, Marian Chalon, Maria Cozzi, Vee Singh, Christine Spiridonos, Maria Tancredi, Ross Buscemi, Panos Kalathas, George Lekakis, Elias Tsigaras, Ilias Tsinanis. I love you guys.

My lifelong friend, Stella Tsikopoulos. In a parallel universe we are in New York City 'strutting unique'. Vicki Boiles, Joanne Cashell, Ham Hatsis, Rita Lunardi, Annie Papadopoulos, my loving sisters and friends, beautiful courageous women.

My God daughter Yanie Drysdale, a compassionate young woman who made it possible for me to become a (sort of) mother.

My extended family Stephie and Nellie Nikoloudis, Julie Lazaridis, Theoni and Chrysoula Parmakellis, Penny and Angelos Apostolou, Maria and Pasquale for their enthusiasm and for listening.

I have been blessed with an amazing family. Marsy, Kim, Anna, BillEye, Anesti Cosmas, I love you more than life itself.

To Prince Rogers Nelson, whose passing propelled me into courageous acts of creativity.

PREFACE

As far back as I can remember I've written things down. As a child, words that sounded funny or looked quirky on paper. As Mum read stories out loud. Quotes, sayings, bits of information I'd hear on the radio, meaning of words I didn't know and journal entries, although, never in a consciously creative way. In 2010, during recovery from a CFS relapse, I made a decision (with my specialist's advice) that I would not be able to return to work in the foreseeable future. This was devastating as social work was so much a part of my identity, my beliefs and values. Writing creatively was something I wanted to explore and so I started writing about issues close to my heart.

This poetry collection came out of a writing challenge I embarked on in 2021. In 2020, a global pandemic challenged the way I interacted with others and the world around me. What did sustain me, however, were Zoom meetings and poetry workshops on line. The poems I wrote reflected the angst, uncertainty and trauma we face collectively. As we endeavour to navigate our way through this time, writing remains an avenue for healing.

'When you depart for Ithaca wish for the road to be long, full of adventure, full of knowledge' Cavafy

1. SEEDS OF SWEET ALYSSUM

Stitched together

this heart threads atoms

a tight knot of molecules

thumps a fight or flight response

Confined to a cheap wooden bed

as tiny cracks splinter

I follow them to the edge

anguish at their escape

Muffled words spoken

in the adjoining room

water poured loudly

blue and white crockery trembles

Episodes of Sex and the City

scene after scene replay

floating gravel in my head

unmoored endings remain

Willing a different outcome

gripping onto a frantic faith

a phony prophet buying time

darkness stokes seeds of sweet
alyssum

I am sundrenched dreams

walking along Elwood beach

seaweed a green algae lace

sea breeze brushing my face

2. SUMMER OF '74

December

sunlight streams into our front room

a woody scent of paper drifts

from a large cardboard box

where piles of books

ordered by colour

entice me to escape

outside a babel of voices

workers swarm like bees

to Richmond station

bright colours scattered

diesel trapped in polyester

they sing harmonies to forget

the whir of the machines

Rosella, Pelaco, Bryant and May

soups, shirts and Redhead boxes

no overtime today

Disney, Grimm and Aesop

Golden Books with thin hard spines

we take turns

my friend and I

I'm Pippi Longstocking

She's Nancy Drew

January

tin roof and weatherboard

a magnet for heat

streets deserted

dry thirsty asphalt

we peer out the window

men with hats stumble home

from quenching a thirst

we catch the train to Sandringham

I pull on my swimsuit

wriggle my feet

deep into the sand

cool and moist

open my book cover

shake the grit from the pages

plunge into my next adventure

3. DUCKS AND A LATTE
@JERRY'S

We walk a leaf-strewn path

wear layers

turn back

grab a scarf

wrap it round

my face and neck

a protective shield

At the canal

grunting ducks

anticipate day old bread

-we feed them

A man pushing a stroller stops

tells us ducks

cannot digest bread

males don't quack

but rasp

a little boy

(we think the pretty child is a girl)

pushes himself up in the stroller

and smiles

People are always friendly

pushing strollers

walking dogs

Runners though

they aren't so friendly

they don't smile

to annoy them

know what I do?

say G'day

stop them to ask the time

I don' wear a watch

I bought a special edition

New York Swatch

at the Swatch store

in Times Square

where it's always busy

There are peaceful districts

in New York

the Flat Iron

in Midtown

One Sunday afternoon

we walk to Eataly (an Italian cafe)

eat gelato

have a real coffee

a rarity in New York

Aussies

opening cafes

New Yorkers love Australians

until recently had no idea

what good coffee was

In Elwood we stop

buy a latte at Jerry's

sit and sip slowly

walk home

Remembering the ducks

I rummage through the pantry

oats and seeds and corn kernels

4. #A LOVE POEM REMADE

ALEXANDRIA PEARY, "THE ARCHITECTURE OF A LOVE POEM"

'Build a wall and keep them out'

brick by brick

iron words can be seen and heard

on FOX news and MAGA (Make America Great Again) caps

in an e-mail, an apology, in a thought about the weather

no immigrants, no climate change, jobs to stay

Standing on a cold morning

in the dole queue with a thermos in hand

you look at the word Love written

on the

wall of an evangelist church and count
the exclusions

because this is where a love poem once
stood

and now panic writes its verses

a love poem, the fossils of a cupola,

preserved in blood red sediment

and three red dots, You, second person
pink

now white and black and supreme white

like in an advent calendar to see

sticker scenes thought long gone

of blacks serving tea and fanning lords

two cups by themselves on a table

ultra white ladies discussing the selling
of slaves

they drink meditative water

their God approving of barbarity

It's now ALL pink rubble, rhyming bricks,
and an illicit balcony

dissent takes place in black and white

it starts to look like a bird cage

trapped canaries singing blues

near springtime-fresh trees,

I hear two people sing

'black and white together we shall not
be moved'

5. AROUND THE CORNER FROM PUNT ROAD

An ambush of yellow and black

men women and children chant

we're from Tiger land

Dad drives a yellow cab at night

Mum whispers look after your brother

she hurries to work pre light

Plastic soldiers lined up ready

war strategy in place

clumsy me then Armageddon

Vegemite sandwiches for lunch

Don't open the door to anyone

Teaspoons of Milo crunch

We buy a colour TV

Batman in blue

bathrobes in pink

Sunday radio blaring

onion frying

a song of home and Mum is crying

On the couch Me and Mum cuddle

Vietnam on the news

Superheros carpet struggle

Brand new lemon tree

next year yellow balls of fruit

manure reeks on patch of dirt

Mum makes me wear a girdle at ten

Keeps your tummy tight

chocolate biscuits on the tram

Get a degree says Mum

don't rely on anyone

will you ever get married?

6. ANTISEPTIC

skies masked in grey

street noise hushed

diesel fumes on hold

coffee aroma lingers

threads its way through ethanol

PRIMAGEL Plus pumped

a doctor in blue garb

his face covered

clean white

Mediterranean hues

I'm feeling the sun

at the elevator

he presses the button

sanitise

doors open

we adjust our masks

no more than four

stand apart

ascending in heady chlorine

third floor

west wing

day procedures

sanitise

in the waiting room a barrier

protects office workers

protects us

new normal a sign signals

every second chair empty

blue curtain

a shield in battle

sanitise

the ward

astringent

medicinal

near empty

once stronger in numbers

now safer alone

limit visits

sanitise

step out

steel blue skies beckon

breathe in the organic air

spicy and resinous

minty and herbaceous

subtle earthy

woody rich

7. CATASTROPHISING

A granny rug wraps me tightly

patches of colour stitched together

hold me against darkness

I stand on the back porch

a bushy tailed possum

stops suddenly

frozen in time

precarious on the wooden fence

I breathe in the cold air

My dreams are lucid

an infant in a facemask

barely a year old she no longer smiles

risk by super spreaders averts eye
contact

parents die while babies nurse on
breasts

a sudden gust forces the branches

against the window

shaken awake to noisy thunder

I pace the hallway in cotton stretch and
runners

repeat yoga poses from a class on line

breathe and hold stretch bend and twist

feel my body expand

my phone pings

my heart races

NEGATIVE in large print

Opening the window I inhale the clean
air

8. FRAGMENTS

air ripe with dewy petrichor

post-rain afternoon

a walk in the park

dogs sniff each other's bottoms

settle on friendship

chattering children

run around high on sugar

stumble and trip

clutch mummy's legs

wailing and wingeing

crocodile tears

cutlery clattering as the table is set

frozen pizza in the oven

TV blaring numbers rising

testing and tracing

clusters and curves

active cases passive carriers

math exercise on line

crayon smears on hallway walls

readers ripped in angst

down the road

locked facility doors

masks and gloves

walking frames wiped every hour

a companion dog whimpers

urinates on the parquetry floor

a grandmother hallucinates

pulls at the tube

argues alone

screams to go home

full moon a midnight blue

9. DISTANCE

confined to our homes

common rules like thread looped firmly

flatten the curve

a ribbed tightly closed weave

it cannot be picked

smooth silky clingy isolation

craft paper embossed shimmers

jigsaw puzzles, board games and math

virtual family visits on Skype

leave house for essentials

a magpie's song

a peppered beard

a covered smile unseen

further north a compound

hours pass in opaque solitude

distancing 1.5 metres difficult

Unauthorized Non Citizens dig

bits of discarded string

barbed wire touches Polaris, Sirius and
Alpha Centauri

a school teacher

a man of faith cries

Inshallah

10. SEPIA STAINED

an heirloom

sepia-stained

fraught with yearning

a ticking fobwatch

images of home

olive trees

ripened figs in August

a woman heavy with child

you never return

a memory remains

the woman clothed in black

the fobwatch passed down

11. THE OCCUPATION

(Lesvos, Greece, 1942)

Artemis is small and nimble

apron loaded with courgettes

pockets crammed with parsley and dill

she takes the back alleyways

stopping at the beachfront

a calm blue palette   a rock ledge

she watches German soldiers dive

Ooh la la

yellow heads bob in the glistering water

Baba's fishing boat nearby idle for years

a memory of tasting sardines

Germans choose who will fish here now

feed the Wehrmacht

she hears footsteps her heart races

Mama's voice echoes

don't draw attention to yourself

move unnoticed child and hurry home

holding her laden apron tight

she nods as she passes uncle
Theodoros

barters figs and firewood at aunt
Rinoulas

picks up chickpeas

(they grind well with coffee beans)

thyme for mama's cough

the clack tap of boots

she turns left to avoid the square

men gather at the Mayor's office

Manolis stands gesturing to Pavlos

she crosses abandoned fields

heads west of the village

few fishing families remain

Baba is waiting outside

mending nets he sighs

at night the kerosene lamp flickers

Baba whispers don't trust anyone paidi
mou

Manolis could be a collaborator

Artemis shakes her head A prodotis?

the splat of a motor vehicle

on bedding knitted together

with fishing net

light out

the three of them wait

12. WAITING FOR TINKY

In the evening he waits

stands at the sink

fills his glass

peers out the window

pauses to hear her bell

an anticipatory meandering

He calls her Tinky

not her real name

we heard someone

over the fence

near the lemon tree

call out Frankie

we're pretty sure that's her

Looking after a feline comes easy to him

I guess that makes me

foster mother to a cat

the neighbour's cat

we saw her two weeks ago

then she disappeared

Fretting now

he sighs

where could she be?

stunned by glaring headlights

hit by a car

maybe she won't come back

maybe she's dead

Shhh!

there is movement

in the tree

he puts his glass down

strides past me

maybe she's back

please let it be her

Tinky! Tinkerbell

13. UNTITLED

Whispers and whistles

words superfluous

children on scooters and bikes

crunching autumn leaves

a church bell

a flourish of notes

a mellifluous voice echos

over the road

a coffee machine whirrs

draws us in

like a tribal drum

buzz of human activity

cloud of smoke wafts

smell of sticky sweet vape

ring tones

jangle of keys

a tiny dog squeaks

vibrant and rich

a community social distancing

14. CATCH UP NEW NORMAL

Saturday night

I prepare for our catch up

cocktail glass upright

double shot vodka,

Cointreau, cranberry juice

a hint of lime

a smoky room

encased in laughter

and music (in my mind from another time)

Alicia Keys sings

about leaving Brooklyn

being inspired

bright lights 'Empire State of Mind'

I throw my Denim blue pantsuit

on white cotton sheets

an elegant Mikimoto pearl

necklace and earrings

mismatched

they make for a funky ensemble

Twenty-three minutes to seven

gulp the drink

pour another

months ago

an eighteen-dollar Cosmo sufficed

at bottle shops

now two for one

free delivery

it's cocktail paradise

Hair iron heats

I apply eye shadow

Mulberry Red lipstick

My bunny soft slippers

on stand by

near the laptop

recent book purchases

stacked for show and tell

Twelve minutes to seven

my hair still frizzy

five minutes to go

get into my outfit

slip on my heels

pour another drink

my hair straight

straight as it's going to get

(I could use a Snap chat filter)

no time for that

I enter Zoom

pout

wait for Kathy to start the meeting

I hear the whirr

a mini drone

outside my window

15. A CURVED LEGACY
(BECOMING 50)

My eyes smile through fine lines

tissue thin intractable

vibrant and myopic

this is how old friends know it is me

My dimples are no longer cute

they sit smugly on my thighs

flabby skin begs to settle in

lines that scream of teenage cries

An Aegean island within

broad shoulders and sunshine

could have been on the Olympic team

I tread water but cannot swim

Shaped like sweet summer fruit

a round belly and supple hips

over ripe and juicy

sugary syrup drips from my lips

Redeemed by long lean fingers

nail beds perfect for polish

my Mother's legacy lingers

16. I CAN'T WRITE

the sweet scent of garlic

infused olive oil

meanders through the house

Mama's in the kitchen making my
favourite

fresh tomatoes, string beans, zucchini

herbs picked from the garden

[a tiny patch of earth not intruded on by
concrete]

it produces parsley, chives and dill

the radio is on too loudly

the song melancholy

I speak loudly

when I ask about her day

Bulgarian feta bought at the deli

the price

pink gardenias flowering

in the garden

my father's cold

He is slouched on the couch

television on too loudly

the commentary negative

Olympiakos is losing

against Barcelona

he snarls

angry that his team is on a losing streak

the room musky 'na hathite'

'get lost' he shouts at the TV

dampness and stale cigarettes

he no longer smokes

in the house

outside two cigarettes a day

he has breakfast

'yia to tsigaro' for the cigarette

he explains to anyone who asks

In my room

a white embroidered cushion

yiayia's contribution to my dowry

on the cluttered mantlepiece

landscapes and faces in frames

the tiny antique table

a cup of coffee

a film of milk

covers the top

jasmine and vanilla

base notes linger

perfume sprayed

a one-way conversation

from the kitchen

the tone harsh

accusatory

an aging conflict

far from settled

a typewriter sits

an old lime laminated table

I sit on a hard wooden chair

the last one standing

I have nothing to write about

17. LAMENT

a sheet covering hangs

without form shaping

the body beneath it-

grey feet are exposed

air heavy

mocks the mother

mourning this loss

silence the voices

loud and relentless

she pleads to those

who won't hear her

the swollen belly

such joy and promise

and here in this noisy

brutal room she knows

darkness covers

the surrounding streets

this day is brief

humid and silver

sandwiched

between two nights

silence

sucking hours

then days

into its cavernous hold.

18. ENCOUNTER

flying past it startles

flirting with my windscreen

black and white and black

weaving in and out

flapping furling furiously

floating feathers

I travel on alone

19. LESS PAINFUL IN PIECES

I remember you in pieces

body parts and silence

less painful this way

Fingers first

long, lean, guitar strumming

lingering on a note

Your eyes follow

dark and persistent

searching

No longer tormenting

I remember you in pieces

less painful this way

20. YOUTH ENDS IN TIME

(for Prince Rogers Nelson)

a name synonymous with youth-

coloured purple

youth euphoric

pushing against the Minnesota wind

your name 0(+>

a symbol of rebellion

bootleg copies selling fast

youthful forceful energy

crushed purple velvet

diamonds and pearls

youth -edgy and energised

it mimics you driving

your red corvette

taking young lovers

eating pancakes

ping pong at midnight

a guitar on standby

the endless corridors

lined with platinum

strutting unique

you remain a mystery

youth - yours and mine

end in time

a sign

youth in that last year

It was let's go crazy

life is a party and it's 1999

it didn't snow in April

that last year of youth